W9-AGD-348

SPICE GIRLS!

SPICE GIRLS!

...AND THEN THERE WERE FOUR

M. Ellen Milner

BARNES
& NOBLE
BOOKS
NEW YORK

This edition published by Barnes & Noble, Inc.
by arrangement with Michael Friedman
Publishing Group, Inc.

1998 Barnes & Noble Books

©1998 by Michael Friedman Publishing Group,
Inc.

All rights reserved. No part of this publication
may be reproduced, stored in a retrieval system,
or transmitted, in any form or by any means,
electronic, mechanical, photocopying, recording,
or otherwise, without prior written permission
from the publisher.

ISBN 0-7607-1169-0

M 10 9 8 7 6 5 4 3 2 1

Art Director: Jeff Batzli
Designer: Lori Thorn
Photography Editor: Valerie E. Kennedy
Production Manager: Susan Kowal

Color separations by Radstock Repro
Printed in England by Butler & Tanner Limited

Every effort has been made to correctly identify
the sources of all the textual and visual material
in this book. The publisher will be happy to cor-
rect any omissions or errors in future editions.

CONTENTS

INTRODUCTION

Spice *n.* 1. a substance that adds strong taste or smell, used for flavoring 2. a thing that adds zest or excitement

Spic*y *adj.* 1. like spice, flavored with spice. 2. slightly scandalous or improper

Girl *n.* 1. a female child 2. a young woman.

Pow*er *n.* 1. the ability to do something. 2. vigor, energy, strength 3. control, influence 4. authority

Travel just a few years back in time and you will find yourself in a world without Girl Power.

Remember? It was a place where the extraordinary young women we now call *Baby*, *Posh*, *Sporty*, *Ginger*, and *Scary* were just girls from England with a really big dream. They rode the London subway. They shopped at the mall. They did their own laundry.

Victoria, Mel C., Emma, Mel B. and Geri pose at London's Heathrow airport.

SpiceFact: It was editors at the British magazine Top of the Pops *who came up with The Girls' nicknames; they published them with an illustration of a spice rack, and press around the world picked up on them.*

The Spice Girls give a high-tech press conference in the spring of 1998.

They rented a dingy little house north of London. Baby and Posh went home most weekends to visit their Moms.

In June 1996, their world changed forever, and so did ours. The day, June 24th to be exact, when Mel C., Mel B., Victoria, Emma, and Geri released their first

single, "Wannabe," appeared on the surface to be a day like any other. In reality, a power had been unleashed that music fans around the globe had been craving. The Girls' trip to the top of the world began almost instantly: In what seemed like a flash, a second on a stop-watch, days filled with movie stars and limousines, film shoots and private jets, weekends in Bali and command performances for the Prince of Wales became as common and ordinary as picking up milk from the corner shop had been just moments before.

What happened?

What happened to them?

What happened to *us*?

This book tells the story.

"I will never forget the day they burst in here. They caused such a commotion, doing a mad routine in the office, all talking at once and being really funny. I called [deputy managing director Ray] Cooper and said, 'You have to see this'."

—Virgin Records Deputy Managing Director, Ashley Newton

"I believe we are the luckiest five girls on earth."

—Mel B.

THE MYTH

According to the official story spun by the press releases that heralded The Spice Girls' takeover of the pop world, Geri Estelle Halliwell (*Ginger Spice*), Victoria Caroline Addams (*Posh Spice*), Melanie Jane Chisholm (*Sporty Spice*), Melanie Janine Brown (*Scary Spice*) and Emma Lee Bunton (*Baby Spice*), are just five hard-working British lasses who struck gold— and then platinum, and then diamonds! Brought together by happenstance—this version says the Girls met at auditions in and around London ("We were the ones who were always rejects but really got on well together," as Victoria Addams tells it)—they began sharing a house in the small town of Maidenhead in 1993. They came from different regions of England, but shared a single dream: to have their own band. They looked each other over and figured out (with a stroke of astonishing brilliance) the hook that would set them apart. By simply accentuating the character- istics already defining who they were, they could create a group that managed to include quali- ties understood by every girl in the world: They would be a little bit sexy yet a touch shy; hip but with a retro feel; homey but with dreams of seeing the world; posh and sophisticated with a dash of country-girl charm; proud, strong, and unafraid to speak their minds. The Girls decided to package themselves as exactly who they were; they would simply erase the day-to-day insecuri- ties that kept them down. Individually, The Girls were just anonymous young women who could sing. Together, they defined the zeitgeist of a generation.

Borrowing cash from Mom and Dad, they set about planning a showcase at Nomis Studios in London. They tinkered with their individual styles, they bought clothes, they practiced. When the pulse felt just right, they invited about twenty company reps from around the UK to see who would bite. Remarkably, that's all it took. The show sent tidal waves of buzz throughout the industry. Phones started ringing. Folks starting talking. In May 1995, just as they had envisioned, The Girls signed a deal with Simon Fuller's *19 Management*, known the world over as the top-notch manager of Annie Lennox.

And the rest, as they say, is history. Or so the story goes.

The truth, as always, is more complicated.

The Spice Girls at the MGM Hotel in Las Vegas, Nevada, for the Billboard Awards in December 1997.

REALITY

In February 1997, an English newspaper, the *Daily Mail*, filled in some of the details The Girls had kept to themselves. In fact, the five friends had received more than a little help along the road to superstardom. Turns out they had met at an audition—an audition sponsored by three men whose plan was to create a girl group, make some fast cash, and retire rich. They were Bob Herbert, his son Chris, and Chic Murphy, the man with the cash who had been around the block and back in the hit-or-miss pop music world. All three men had had a taste of the heady possibilities of the biz—Herbert with a "here today, gone tomorrow" British boy band imaginatively called Bros, and Murphy with a seventies girl soul group, The Three Degrees. With the new band they hoped to hit the big time.

More than 600 young women hungry for stardom responded to the ad the three ran in the theater magazine, *The Stage*. The ad was placed in a theater rag because the men were looking for girls with more than just good singing voices. They wanted *presence*, the kind of talent you find

Dressed in sexy pinstripes, The Girls arrive for the world premiere of *Spiceworld* in London.

In February 1998, The Girls celebrated Victoria's engagement to soccer star David Beckham.

in theater. They were searching for girls with personality, who could belt out a song and act as well—young women who each showed potential star power, but who at the same time accentuated each other's differences. The only thing they would need to share was a blinding desire to succeed. Anything the girls didn't know, the three image-makers figured they could teach. Victoria Addams, Geri Halliwell, Melanie Chisholm, and Melanie Brown made the cut. And so did a girl named Michelle.

Who?

Michelle learned quickly that she wasn't cut out for the Spice Girl world.

At the start of the experiment, and for many months to come, it wasn't a glamorous existence. The girls were put up in a house in Maidenhead, their basic expenses were paid, and their transformation began. No one could play an instrument well (Victoria could hit a few notes on a keyboard and Geri could strum the guitar "very badly") and the five had voices that would do—Annie Lennox they weren't. Their lives became a daily round of singing lessons, social training, and image sharpening. Their first voice coach, Pepi Lemer, recalled for the *Daily Mail* her thoughts when she was first introduced to the fledgling stars: "I remember them being attractive in their different ways but terribly nervous. They were shaking and when they sang

16

"*R.U. 18–23 with the ability to sing/dance? R.U. streetwise, outgoing, ambitious, and dedicated?*"

—from the ad placed in *The Stage*

The Spice Girls fooling around at America Online, where they chatted live with fans in May 1997.

their voices were wobbling….My first impression was 'My God, there's a lot of work to be done here.'" Within a few months, Michelle had had enough and quit. She was soon replaced by Emma Bunton. The five were putting in long, hard, exhausting days but improvement began to come. Ever so slowly, The Spice Girls as we know them were beginning to take shape.

In the UK and to a lesser degree in North America, manufacturing bands is an ancient music industry rite. Even The Beatles, arrived in the United States to appear on "The Ed Sullivan Show" sporting identical haircuts, matching suits, and a marketing plan. Pulling up the rear in the "manufactured band" spectrum, The Bay City Rollers, a British pop sensation of the seventies, were packaged in horrific tartan pants (riding high above their ankles for some bizarre and ill-conceived reason), which soon became a fashion craze as the boys rode the wave of their one zippy little hit, *Saturday Night* and then retreated forevermore into the shade of "Whatever Happened to ?" newspaper columns the world over. Somewhere between these two possibilities lay the future of the five girls in Maidenhead.

The first glimmer of what would set them apart began to appear in early 1995. As their confidence in their singing and dancing grew, so did the realization that their faith in the truth of their so-called package was absolute. After all, the core element of the group's potential power out there in the real world was something very tangible: It was *them*! Geri, then known as "Sexy Spice," really was a good-hearted vamp, but she was also strong-willed, disciplined, used to working hard and blessed with a mind of her own. Victoria was Posh! She loved Gucci and Prada and was willing to work eighteen-hour days to afford their charge cards on her own. Emma Bunton was the baby of the group, and she could bat her eyes to get the things she really wanted in life. Yes, she was cute and blond and bubbly, but she was also a playful mix of fascinating contradictions—she had a blue belt in Goju, a type of karate, for goodness sake! Melanie B. was Scary—but only to people inclined to wimpiness. Her scariness was the best kind—her drive was scary, her ability to talk truth was scary, her willingness to go the extra mile was scary. Melanie C. was sporty, the kind of girl who feels rotten all day if she doesn't work out first thing in the morning.

Promoting their big-screen debut in *Spiceworld,* The Girls glam it up at Cannes.

So did it matter if the true stories of their lives included some dark patches hidden away in corners? They were real, and they had faith in themselves, not just in *the package*.

After months of being managed, The Girls began to realize they wanted some control. Handing the entirety of their lives and careers over to "packagers" seemed to them more frightening than fighting for the right to have input into the direction they were traveling. They knew they needed help—with music, with arrangements, with deal-making—and they weren't afraid to ask for it. They also believed, at some deeper level, that their own combined wills could be a significant source of creative and business power, if they could only tap that resource.

SPICEQUOTES:

"We never mean to offend anybody, we're just a bit naughty."
—Mel C.

"Every girl's got a right to stick up for herself."
—Mel B.

"I'd like to be remembered as a wild freedom fighter with a method to her madness."
—Geri

"We're not claiming to be soul divas, we're just having a laugh."
—Victoria

"If I wasn't in the Spice Girls, I'd probably be a cashier."
—Emma

TAKING CONTROL

Here's where the myth and reality cross paths. At this point, it was growing obvious that the packagers and The Girls wanted the band to move in different directions—the men wanted the band to behave as an all-girl version of The Monkeys: Do what they were told, sing the songs picked for them, trust the boys to manage this adventure as they saw fit, don't ask too many questions. Everything would work out if they tried a little harder to be happy being treated like little girls.

Sadly, the guys didn't understand what they had created. Spending time together, getting to know each other, learning they actually had something to say, The Girls started to imagine their own future. They pulled together with an "all for one and one for all" sort of power and went for it—and they negotiated their way out of the contract they had signed. And they set up that meeting with Simon Fuller at 19 Management..."Simon was really cool," remembers Melanie B. "We had so many managers saying 'dress like this, sing that song, I can make you big stars.' Simon was really laid back and understood we wanted a say in how our careers would go."

They signed on with Simon and starting shopping for a record deal.

As Mel B. says, " You can do what you want in

this group, it's great! You can be as mad as you want, as normal as you want, or as loud or as proud as you want!"

As long as we're having fun, that's the whole vibe of it all. Do you know what I mean? We're doing this 'cause we enjoy it and it's a lifestyle and it's a wicked career, and we're making our own decisions and hopefully we're giving a positive message to anyone who'll listen.

—interview with MTV's Kurt Loder

Who would have believed it? The Spice Girls holding their 1998 Brit Award for outstanding LP sales.

In fairness, The Girls had to acknowledge that the Herberts and Murphy had indeed paved the way. By this point, the men's scheme had started to pay off and there was a buzz in the industry about an interesting all-girl pop band looking for a contract. Then, with Simon's impeccable connections and astute understanding of the game, the roller coaster ride to success began in earnest.

Interest from record companies led to a series of meetings. Most of the time, The Girls were bombarded with more of the same type of superficial advice they'd been hearing for so long—about what to wear and how to cut their hair. Most executives couldn't seem to understand that what they saw and heard was what they were going to get.

Finally, The Girls met the folks at Virgin Records. These guys got it: and they liked what they saw and liked what they heard. At The time, Virgin Managing Director Newton was quoted: "Historically, our acts have come out of left field and ended up in the mainstream. But it is an indication of how Virgin is broadening that we would take on The Spice Girls—they've got credibility and are a convincing pop act. Their music is bright and sexy, and they have a spirit of camaraderie. They draw on certain soul traditions and as an old soul boy, I couldn't resist." At Virgin, the girls had found a home, a place where they were respected for being who they were. They signed.

The Girls were finally on their way.

"When I was little I always thought, 'I want to be famous.' But you could never dream about what has happened to us."

—Victoria Addams

"Taking on the British pop boys, just when boys with guitars threaten to rule pop life—Damon's all over with 'Smash Hits,' Ash are big in 'Big,' and Liam can't move for tabloid frenzy—an all-girl, in-yer-face pop group have arrived with enough sass to burst that rockist bubble."

—dotmusic

"The boys with guitars had better prepare for battle..."

—MusicWeek

THE MUSIC

All the pieces were falling into place. The Girls had signed with one of the most important record companies in the world. They had inked a publishing deal. They had polished their singing and dancing talents. They had learned how to eat smoked salmon. They had acquired the skills to deal with important and powerful people in the business with stylish aplomb. They knew who they were and what they wanted to say.

What they didn't have was a record.

No matter how great the expectations, no matter how confident Fuller and Virgin were about the future, The Girls knew the bottom line would be the music. If an audience wasn't singing along, snapping their fingers to the beat, all The Girls' hard work would be for naught. If they didn't cut the mustard where it mattered most, it was going to be "well, that was fun for a while, now let's get a job at the mall" time. So they hunkered down and got to work.

No one had ever pretended that The Girls were virtuoso musicians. Neither were they professional songwriters. They could, and did, write, but they needed the help of pros, those musical craftsmen with years of experience, to shape their instincts and ideas into songs with number-one hit potential. The Girls found their boys in production duo Andy Watkins and Paul Wilson (aka Absolute.) Watkins and Wilson proved masterful at taking The Girls' words, polishing them, adding beat and jive, and creating tunes like the unforgettable "Something Kinda Funny." Geri recalled later the song was a "… reflection of what was going on with us at the time….Remember to enjoy the adventure, the journey—it's just as important as when you arrive."

The Girls also turned to the team of Richard Stannard and Matt Rowe, studio pro-

Mel B. in fringe and Baby in a sheer dress— hanging at Heathrow.

ducers who worked under the delightful name of Biff 'n' Memphis. "We didn't want a run-of-the-mill producer," Geri remembers. "We worked with soul boys and remixers who were undiscovered and open to letting us lean over their shoulder and say 'Would you turn up that bass line,' or 'Would you put a little more EQ [equalization] on that vocal.'" Pretty soon The Girls had thirty songs ready to go and had established a smooth, tight working relationship with their team. Speaking after the Girls had launched, Richard Stannard said: "I think their appeal is such that people initially think, 'Hang on, this is a manufactured band.' But everything was there right from the beginning— the attitude, the philosophy, the 'Girl Power' thing…they had all the ideas for the songs and

Mel B. wears white and Victoria a fur-trimmed coat as they head off to America.

we'd sort of piece them together like a jigsaw puzzle." After endless days and nights of writing, rewriting, and polishing; of throwing songs away and bringing them back again, fourteen songs made the final cut. On the morning The Spice Girls arrived at the Olympic studio, a huge recording space in Central London that had seen thousands of musicians walk through its doors, little did anyone know they were taking one step closer to the brink of pop-music history. But they were hoping.

Months of work followed. The vocal tracks were recorded—and then mixed and remixed and mixed again, at scores of other state-of-the-art spots in and around London. No detail was forgotten or overlooked. They had come too far to forget about being perfectionists now. At last the tapes were delivered to Virgin. Mel C., Mel. B., Victoria, Emma, and Geri waited for the word with fingers crossed. Their talent may be old news now, but at the time, The Spice Girls desperately needed the reassurance.

Finally, the word came from Virgin: a huge thumbs-up. The launch plan was rushed into place. The Spice Girls would be introduced to the media in April 1996 and the first single would be released in June. There was no looking back now.

An imaginary day in the life of The Spice Girls, *Spiceworld* shows girl power

Reviews of *Spiceworld*:

"Spiceworld is...big, jiggly fun." —**Toronto Star**

"A candy-colored, scantily-clad, 007-style romp."

—**Entertainment Weekly**

in action against such characters as a manipulative manager, a greedy Hollywood producer, and a persistent paparazzo.

Baby in blue—Emma helps to Spice up the crowd at Wembley Stadium in April 1998.

The Spice Bus takes The Girls on a wild ride in *Spiceworld*.

Spiceworld: The Movie offers a day-in-the-life of our favorite girls as they pre-pare for their first concert, to be held at Royal Albert Hall. We follow The Girls around London in the Spice Mobile, a double-decker bus painted like the Union Jack, as they are pursued by various villainous media types, including a British tabloid editor who hires a reporter to try to catch The Girls doing naughty things; a documentarian who wants to capture the "essence" of Spice; and a greedy Hollywood producer.

The very funny Richard E. Grant plays their neurotic manager, while Roger Moore is "The Chief," a record company executive who wears silk robes and ascots. The bus driver is played by Meatloaf, and George Wendt of Cheers fame is the Hollywood producer. Stars such as Elton John, Bob Geldof, and Elvis Costello show up in cameos. There is even a visit from aliens, who are thrilled to get a kiss from Ginger!

The Girls had so much fun making the movie that they are planning to film another at the end of 1998. Victoria says she's game, "As long as it's a glamorous role," and the other Girls say they just want to have fun!

CHANGING THE WORLD FOREVER

Once the marketing machine starts rolling, there's no stopping it, especially when the crowds are picking up the scent of a hit in the air. And in April and May there was a strong whiff of success in the air at the Virgin headquarters: What no one realized at the time was that The Spice Girls were about to conquer not only the United Kingdom, but the world.

The Girls had no time to be nervous. Once the recordings were completed, there were more dance moves to learn, clothes to buy, photo sessions to attend, videos to make for the release of "Wannabe," not to mention strategic interviews to give. The Girls went on a press junket, meeting and greeting the media writers and radio hosts who would decide how often their songs would be played on air and, to some extent, how they would be received. The Girls talked about their

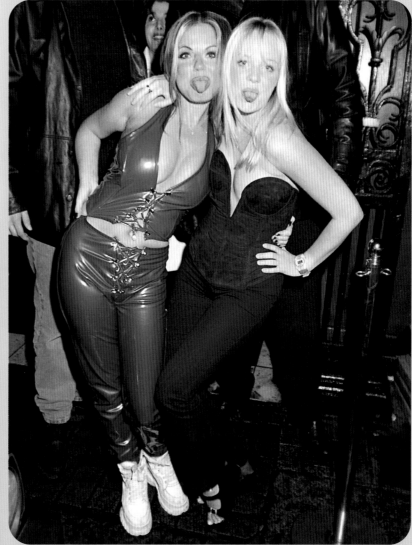

Left: Followed everywhere by reporters, The Girls figure they might as well make it a good time! Above: Ginger and Baby show their disdain for the paparazzi.

> *"When we write, you know, we write about things we feel passionately about and our real life experiences. So when we write it's a real vibe thing, we get in the studio and we throw ideas around."*
>
> **—interview with MTV's Kurt Loder**

influences and their hopes: "We want to bring some glamour back to pop," Geri told *dotmusic*, "like Madonna when we were growing up. Pop is about fantasy and escapism, but there's so much bull-shit around at the moment. We want to be relevant to girls our age." Melanie B. joined in: "Remember when Neneh first appeared on the scene? She was a ballsy, sexy woman from out of nowhere with a completely new attitude."

The Spice Girls were introduced to the public on a British cable music show called "The Box." People started phoning in at once—Who were these girls? Where could fans buy the song? The reaction was phe-nomenal. It was still two weeks before the official release but all the signs just kept get-ting better and better. The Girls did another blitz of interviews, singing *a cappella* in cramped little radio station studios, goofing around with the hosts, getting the word out. By the time they did a series of more in-depth spots on Radio One stations during the final week of advance media, it felt like The Spice Girls might just take the UK by storm.

In fact, it was more like a hurricane.

Within weeks of its release, record stores couldn't keep "Wannabe" on the shelves. The Spice Girls were everywhere. The video was being played almost every hour on British MTV. Overnight it seemed that the entire country had figured out what they collectively really, really wanted—more of The Spice Girls!

"If you wanna be my lover, you gotta get with my friends,
Make it last forever, friendship never ends."

—**"Wannabe," from *Spice***

Celebrating another award at the Fourth Annual MTV Europe Music Awards, held in the Netherlands in November 1997.

CHAPTER THREE

THE VIBE

IS CONTAGIOUS...

"We're the Spice Girls, ready to go, ladies and gents, can you please take your seats, and we hope that you enjoy the show!"

—"The Lady is a Vamp," *Spiceworld*

The Spice Girls' dreams came true in what seemed like seconds. "Wannabe" catapulted to the number one spot on the charts. As did the next single, "Say You'll Be There," followed by the next two singles. In no time at all, The Girls were number one in the United Kingdom, Demark, Japan, and Turkey! Then The Girls took on America—and repeated their triumph: With three singles in the top ten, *Spice* sold more than five million copies in the U.S. alone.

By late 1997, The Girls' movie, *Spiceworld*, was an international blockbuster, and the second album went platinum. A world tour was planned for 1998. And then things started to change.

Prince Charles looks bemused by the attentions of The Girls—Geri actually pinched his bottom!

In November 1997, The Girls fired their manager, Simon Fuller, and took full control of their own careers. Geri had figured out that Simon was taking a bigger slice of the Spice pie than The Girls were receiving themselves: It just didn't make financial sense. As the months passed, Geri assumed a larger role in The Spice Girls' business empire...but tensions began to grow.

And then came the blow-up. According to their chauffeur, a fight had been brewing for weeks. Rumors were flying of an affair between Emma and Simon Fuller; Geri was making more and more of the decisions; and the old difficulties between Geri and some of the other girls re-emerged. Things turned sour the week of May 24, 1998, while the group was on the first leg of their world tour. Exhausted by the show in Helsinki, Ginger and the others began fighting in the car on the way to the airport, and continued their argument in the VIP lounge. The teary battle accelerated aboard the private jet, and upon touchdown at Heathrow, Geri stormed off, furious at what she felt was a lack of respect.

The next day, Geri failed to show up for a London television show taping, claiming illness. The next day, she missed the show in Oslo, leaving the four other girls to perform without her. The world press jumped on the story immediately. On Saturday, May 30, 1998, newspapers around the world reported, as did New York's *Daily News*, that there was "Trouble in Para-Spice."

Victoria tried to quash the rumors, telling reporters, "Right now Geri is sick and tired. She's just reached the limit. We are not splitting up." But on Sunday, Ginger released her own statement: "Sadly, I would like to confirm that I have left The Spice Girls because of differences between us. I am sure the group will be successful and I wish them all the best. P.S. I'll be back."

Fans worldwide reacted with shock—particularly the Canadian and American Spice fans holding tickets for the upcoming North American leg of the world tour. Posh, Baby, Sporty, and Scary responded immediately: "We are sorry to all our fans for having to go through all this. We are upset and saddened by Geri's departure, but are very supportive in whatever she wants to do. Friendship never ends....The Spice Girls are here to stay, see you at the stadiums!"

And so the four remaining Spices strengthened their bonds and went on with the show, wowing audiences and showing that girl power is strong even in the face of adversity.

Melanie Jane Chisholm
SPORTY SPICE

Born: January 12, 1974

Quirky characteristics: A nose ring, and two tattoos: the Japanese characters for woman and strength on her shoulder and a Celtic band tattooed on her right arm.

What's your favorite saying?

"You'll never walk alone."

How do you win an argument?

"I deck 'em."

How do you meet guys?

"I give them a shy glance then flex my biceps. I'd chat him up with 'I've got two tickets for a Liverpool match, do you fancy coming?'"

What about [public] toilet hygiene?

"Me? I use the urinals, mate!"

What do you do before bedtime?

"I do fifty stomach crunches."

Three Rules to Live By:

- Try and beat the boys at their own game and don't give in. If you can't beat them, join them.

Mel C. at the Polaroid Spicecam publicity shoot.

- Eat a healthy diet and listen to your body. But don't bother dieting—it doesn't work.

- Do exactly what you want to do and don't let anyone tell you otherwise.

—from the Official Spice Girls Website

On the surface Melanie C. can seem like the odd girl out. She wouldn't be caught dead in a short skirt. She doesn't need to be wearing mascara when she runs out to buy some tea at the corner store. She can think of no better way to

Mel C. previously worked as a session singer, and says the studio is her favorite place. Track suits and comfy clothes are what you'll find her dressed in!

Sporty's nickname couldn't be more suitable. She says she can't do without the gym, "If I'm not running, I'm pressing weights."

spend a Saturday night than with a few of her best mates from home watching the Liverpool soccer team win on their home turf. In the old days, she would have been called a tomboy. Today she's called Sporty Spice.

And she is seriously sporty. The first thing she does in the morning is work out, and work out is the last thing she does at night before going to bed. It calms her, eases the stress of her unforgiving schedule as a Spice Girl, and keeps her body buff, something she is very proud of. Her eyes glint with pleasure every time she flexes her biceps.

Born in Liverpool in the north of England, Melanie C.'s heart remains there. She was the only daughter (she has two brothers) of a part-time singer and an elevator repairman. Both her parents loved the music scene of Liverpool—in fact, they met at the Cavern Club, where the most famous of

"I love exercise, and I go to the gym a lot, but I still find that one of the best ways to exercise is to put on my favorite tunes and jump around like a nutter."—Mel C.

Mel C. told her fans at AOL that for her, girl power means "accepting yourself, learning to love yourself and being a strong female. And not taking any rubbish from men!"

Sporty started doing gymnastics at age eight.

Liverpool bands, The Beatles, got their start. Her parents divorced when she was still a child, and the kids and their mom, Joan, moved to Widness, a small industrial town where Joan could find work.

Melanie remembers her childhood as an endless search for a place she could feel comfortable and truly be herself. She never really felt she was fitting in. "I always ended up playing a sheep in the Nativity play while the other girls dressed like angels." She studied ballet and acted but spent more time working at a fish and

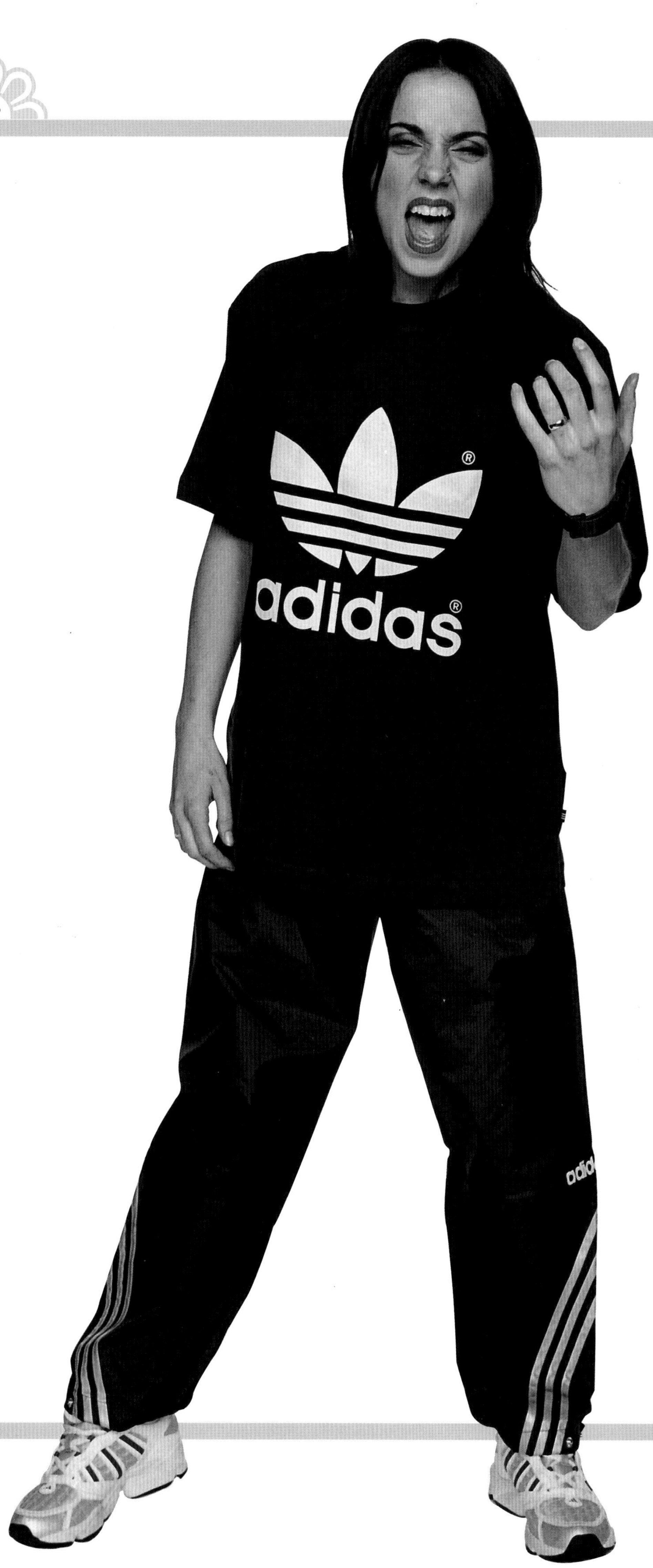
adidas

Emma and Mel C. are great friends. Baby says of Sporty, "She's a cool chick."

chip shop than she did tuning her talents on a stage. Only when she moved to London and met

her future Spice sisters at the audition did she find the place where she could shine for who she

really was—a sports fanatic who could sing!

In the group, Melanie is the one who always wants to be up and doing something. During

the shooting of *Spiceworld*, Melanie was the one who was most frustrated by waiting around,

hour after hour, for filming to begin. Emma says: "She's a very funny person when you talk to

her, and when she's got something to say, it's very important. And she gets us all up and going

when we've been a bit...saying "Come on now, we've got a singing lesson, or we've got a

dance lesson."

Melanie Janine Brown
SCARY SPICE

Born: May 29, 1975

Quirky characteristics: A pierced tongue and eyebrow

What's your favorite saying?

"Get 'em out for the lasses!"

How do you win an argument?

"Shout and shout and shout more…even when they have gone."

How do you meet guys?"

"No hesitation, I'd bowl over to him and tell him I fancy him. I'd chat him up with 'Forget the small talk, what's your….?'"

What about [public] toilet hygiene?

"I don't go!"

What do you do before bedtime?

"I fall down in a comfy position anywhere."

Three Rules to Live By:

• Tell him/her you fancy them. You've got nothing to lose.

• Be proud of your race and color—it's who you are.

• Be as outrageous and as mad as you possibly can, even if you are by yourself.

—from the Official Spice Girls website

Mel B. looks great even when she's running to catch a plane! She flashes a victory sign at Heathrow Airport in January 1997.

Melanie B. has been called "the loudest and most upfront example of girl power in action." She's strong-willed, unafraid to speak her mind, and loves the spotlight. From her zebra suits and hot pants to her pierced tongue and flying hair, Melanie is a whirlwind of personality. In the beginning, back during the days in the house at Maidenhead, Mel B. and Geri had a quite a few run-ins. Both strong and opinionated, they needed some time to figure out that they could each get what they wanted and still be friends. In the good old days, Scary and Ginger seemed to work off each other to keep the others in line: "Me and Geri lay down the law. I do the brutal attack while Geri is fair and listens to both sides of the story." These days, rumor has it that

Many of the costumes Scary wears she designs herself. A multitalented Girl, she played drums, danced, did telephone sales, and had a brief stint on the British TV soap *Coronation Street* before becoming a Spice.

Asked about her fears by a fan on AOL, Mel B. replied, "I don't dread anything in life aside from toe sucking."

it was a huge Ginger/Scary blow-up that finally helped push Ginger over the edge...but Mel B. doesn't apologize for her strong personality.

Mel B. is the Spice with a strongest sense of urban style. From her funky glasses to the tip of her platform boots, she seems to define hip. She loves London's club scene, and dancing till dawn. Victoria says "Mel B. is the ultimate Spice girl—pretty, clever, crazy, and impudent."

Melanie's dad came to England from the West Indies, where he met her mother, a local girl named Andrea. They fell in love and married at a

Mel B. loves to wear leopard prints, and confides "I'm into leopard nail art, it's kickin'!!"

On her days off, Mel reports that she's either "chilling out or partying," because she is "an extreme kind of gal."

time when interracial marriages were less common than they are now. Rather than be ashamed of her background—and there were lots of ignorant kids and families in town who would have preferred if she were—Mel B. was raised to feel beautiful and special. Her background did cause some confusion: "My surname is Brown and I thought when I was really young that I was called Brown because I am brown. I wasn't black and I wasn't white. And I couldn't understand why so-and-so wasn't called White."

Mel B. got engaged to dancer Jimmy Gulzar in June 1998, after a whirlwind romance. (He performed as her shadow "Spice Boy" on the world tour.) But Mel B. doesn't think love will change her views: "Some of us have boyfriends, but men don't rule our lives. They should be like mates and should never try to come between you and your mates." Mel B. is intent upon enjoying every new challenge the day brings her. "We're revitalizing pop. Our songs are pop with intelligence and personality....None of our songs are about wishy-washy love".

Scary Spice is a vibrant performer. Here she struts her stuff at a live performance in America.

Mel B. is spontaneous and outrageous in life as well as performance; she says whatever comes to mind!

Victoria Addams
POSH SPICE

Born: April 7, 1975

Quirky characteristics: None. Quirky isn't posh.

What is your favorite saying?

"Do it with style!"

How do you win an argument?

"I give a look that would kill, then I walk away."

How do you meet guys?

"I play it cool and pose. I'd chat him up with 'Is that a designer suit you're wearing?'"

What about [public] toilet hygiene?

"I crouch to avoid contact with the seat!"

What do you do before bedtime?

"I have a full facial routine and put on my silk pajamas!"

Three Rules to Live By:

• If you are going to kiss a boy, make sure you are wearing stay-on lipstick.

• Having an off day? Slap on some lipstick and a pair of shades.

• If you haven't got it, fake it! Too short? Wear big high heels, but do practice walking.

—from the Official Spice Girls website

Victoria winks for reporters outside the MTV Europe Awards.

Posh told online fans that she loves pets, and has three Yorkshire terriers, Lucy, Bambi, and Tiger.

Posh spends her spare time shopping.

Victoria Addams is the sultry Spice, always draped in exquisite clothes and dripping a kind of all-encompassing composure. Even onstage, she exudes class and just a hint of hidden depths raging beneath the surface. She's been called the "ultimate Gucci girl." The truth is, she is exactly who she appears to be—except she's shy, not aloof, something she is often accused of. "Everyone seems to think that I'm majorly moody and I don't ever speak and I've got no personality."

She grew up in an affluent area outside of London, the daughter of a successful businessman and his stay-at-home wife. Her parents believed in supporting their daughter's dreams. Even with all her parents' help, Victoria, like a few of the other girls in the band, never really felt a part of the crowd. It was at college that her shyness fell away. There she met girls who shared her dreams, who she could talk to, and just as importantly, chums to go clubbing

Emma and Victoria accepting The Spice Girls' Brit Award in February 1997.

Sporting her diamond solitaire ring, Posh announces her engagement to soccer star David Beckham in London.

with, even though to this day she rarely drinks. Her confidence in her abilities was strong when she graduated. Even so, she found it tough to land a job. She was going to every audition she possibly could when she stumbled into the Spice Girl try-outs.

Victoria willingly admits that in the beginning, she sometimes found the Spice Girl regimen tough. She was as talented as the others, and willing to work as hard, but unlike most of the girls, Victoria was happy to go home on the weekends and hang around with her family, to which she is still very close. Geri and Mel B. teased her endlessly. As they shared more secrets and spent more time together, the girls worked out their differences and Posh found her place.

The biggest news in Victoria's life these days is her upcoming marriage to Manchester United Soccer star David Beckham. David and Victoria became engaged in February 1998, when David gave his girlfriend a diamond solitaire ring.

Talented and smart, Victoria is also hardworking. She trained at a theatre school, started dancing at the age of three, and always got good grades.

In an early publicity shot Posh struts the haughty look that became her byline.

Some of Victoria's favorite parts of being a Spice Girl: "Traveling the world, meeting some fantastic people. Having fun and doing what I most enjoy."

Emma Bunton
BABY SPICE

Born: January 21, 1976

Quirky characteristics: She looks great with her hair in pig-tails!

What is your favorite saying?

"Home is where the heart is."

How do you win an argument?

"I shed a tear for sympathy."

How do you meet guys?

"I smile sweetly and play with my pig-tails. I'd chat him up with 'Would you like one of my Bon Bons?'"

What about [public] toilet hygiene?

"I always clean before sitting."

What do you do before bedtime?

"I have a last minute cuddle with whoever is next to me!"

Three Rules to Live By:

• Listen to and trust your Mum's advice. At the end of the day she's your best friend.

• Have a boyfriend if he is worth it, but don't let him take you for granted.

Baby loves to bring her stuffed animals everywhere she goes.

• Love yourself for what you are, don't change for anybody … just be who you wanna be.

—from the Official Spice Girls website

Baby sets off on a trip.

Emma Bunton's life changed the day her voice coach from high school looked up her name in the phone book and gave her an unexpected call. Pepi Lemer was whipping the newly formed Spice Girls' voices into shape and number five had just dropped out of the group. Pepi remembered Emma as charming, hard-working and worth a try. Emma's mother took the call and her daughter's life changed forever.

Emma fit in immediately and was soon nicknamed "Baby" because she was the youngest, and because she visited her Mother whenever she could. The other girls teased Emma, until they realized just how important

Baby Spice loves all things sweet—from cotton candy to donuts. She told her AOL fans, "My favorite donut is Dunkin' Donuts Boston Creme."

the relationship was to Emma. The band's song "Mama" was written mostly by Emma and she says her eyes well up with tears every time the band sings it! To this day, even when she is on tour halfway around the world or on the set of a movie, she will call her mother—up to three times a day—just to check in.

Baby trying to look sweet and innocent despite a see-through dress. Nice underwear!

Emma dresses like a sexy pixie—wearing babydoll dresses, tying her hair in pigtails, and carrying a teddy bear knapsack. In truth, she is a prankster and isn't above batting her blue eyes to get herself out of a tight corner. She loves her new life but sometimes finds the schedule exhausting. "I'm the kind of person who likes getting up late and going to bed late," she says, which makes getting up at 5:30 am for a film shoot quite a challenge!

Emma loves to sing: "Going into the studio is one of my favorite parts of what we do. I'd done some singing for TV adverts, but it was very exciting doing it for the first time with a band. It's just you and the mike and you're live. When I sing I always shut my eyes to get into the mood and the feeling of the song."

Emma sings a solo at Wembley Stadium in London.

Baby Spice performing "Wannabe" at the Brit Awards in 1998. Baby started singing when she was just a young girl, and began performing in shows when she was eight years old!

Emma hams it up in an early
publicity shot. The final
Spice to join the group, she
got called Baby because
"I'm the youngest. And
because I've got a cute
smile."

Geraldine Estelle Halliwell

EX-SPICE *Goodbye, Ginger Spice*

Born: August 6, 1972

Quirky characteristics: Flaming red hair and a pierced belly button.

What's your favorite saying?

"This is what we're going to do…"

How do you win an argument?

"I throw in a lot of big words and a lot of verbal to confuse the situation…"

How do you meet guys?

"I go for eye-to-eye contact then I lunge. I'd chat him up with 'Hey Mr. Scorpio, here's 10p…call your Mum 'cos you're not going home tonight.'"

What about [public] toilet hygiene?

"I put a pattern of toilet paper down first!"

What do you do before bedtime?

"Plan the next day."

Three Rules to Live By:

• If you have something to say, SAY IT. It's better out than in.

• Personality is like a muscle … use it a lot and it grows and improves.

• Beauty doesn't last. Rely on it and you become cabbage from within.

—from the Official Spice Girls website

Ginger arriving to perform live before The Prince of Wales at The Prince's Trust Concert in London.

Geri's the oldest Spice and, some say, the sexiest, which she herself finds ridiculous. "It's hilarious," she has said. "I'm like any other woman in the world...I'm clumsy, not sexy...I have the same insecurities most women have...but I like that about all of us. We're proof that you don't have to be classically beautiful or six feet tall to be considered attractive...Hopefully we're role models for young girls because of that."

Geri's Mom, who is from Spain, moved to England when Geri was very young. Her father soon left, forcing Geri's Mom to work as an au pair—and to this day she works, most recently as a cleaner in Watford's Harelquin Center, a job she refuses to quit even though her daughter keeps asking her to. As for her childhood, Geri is nonchalant: "The old-fashioned Victorian family of two-point-four kids is dead. But every child needs one decent parent and must learn honest openness about sex, and tolerance."

Far left: Ginger, tanned and happy, poses for the cameras at the Cannes Film Festival in 1997, after The Spice Girls announced their film. Left: Ginger designed the "Cool Britannia" outfit she wore to the Brit Awards in 1997.

> "Of course there's more to me than what gets written, but at the end of the day it's very hard for the media, as a male-dominated industry, to digest the fact that a girl with a pair of big boobs has got a brain."
>
> —Geri, *Interview*, "The Spice Age"

Geri poses with her mother Greta and boyfriend Jamie Morrison.

Geri's life was a series of ups and downs and struggles to find work before she showed up for the audition that would change everything. Her pre-Spice life included jobs as a cleaning lady and as an announcer on a Turkish TV show. The downs were revealed almost as soon as the Spice Girls struck it big. The British tabloids, ever eager to sniff through the underwear

Ginger pretending to be just another sweet little schoolgirl.

drawers of anyone famous, discovered that Geri had posed topless. In a flash the scandal was front page news. To her credit, Geri didn't deny the stories and she didn't run away. She stood her ground: "I'm twenty-four and it's obvious, especially with my background, I haven't gone the clean-cut way. I try to see the positive. Some of the men...well, I might be getting their attention and they might start listening to the music. Get some messages out. Talk about safe sex." Rather than allow a bit of bad press to destroy her career, she owned up to her past, told the truth and was voted the most popular Spice by the British public in response (per a poll conducted by the British magazine *Sky International*.)

Ginger was so popular, in fact, that in May 1998, she decided that a solo career was the next thing she wanted on her resume! In November 1997, Geri had convinced the other girls that Simon Fuller was ripping them off, and he was fired. From then on, every Spice decision was voted on by The Girls themselves. This added responsibility, combined with endless touring and appearances, sponsorships, and recording sessions, took its toll. Geri assumed more and more of the nitty-gritty business responsibilities and felt that the others weren't respecting her hard work. Feeling exhausted, overburdened, and under-appreciated, Geri quit the band.

Before becoming The Girls' resident rapper, she was a model, a barmaid, an aerobics instructor, and a presenter on Turkish television.

CONCLUSION

How did the Spice Girls accomplish so much?

What did they have that set them apart?

In a word, themselves.

The Spice Girls hit because the world was ready for them—for their music and their message. Young women the world over, women who didn't share a language or a country, were craving the same thing: Role models who could giggle and have a good time, yet were strong enough to live life on their own terms. "Girl Power" as the Spice Girls tell it, means a lot of things—be who you are, never sell yourself short, don't do anything you feel uncomfortable doing, live your dreams, work hard, have a good time, and wear platform shoes, short skirts, and nose rings if you want to. Or don't. Just be yourself with all the energy you can muster. Boys are fun and dating is a blast, but boys shouldn't be the be-all and end-all of a girl's day. Getting what you want should be! The Spice Girls keep reminding their fans that every dream can come true—as their own stories prove.

The only person who can stand in your way is yourself.

Girl Power!

MORE INFORMATION ON THE SPICE GIRLS

Are you a passionate Spice Girl fan? The World Wide Web offers lots of sites where you can get more info on The Girls, their music, their tours, and their upcoming projects.

The Official Spice Girls Site at Virgin Records, The Spice Station: http://c3.vmg.co.uk/spicegirls/
Unofficial Sites: Spicegirls.com: www.spicegirls.com/
Spice Girls SuperSite: www. superspice.home. ml.org
Spice Paradise: www.geocities.com/Broadway/Alley/7309?index.html
Spice Shack: www.web.online.co.uk?members/gary.fenton/
Spice Girls NewsCenter: members@aol.com.stondspice/spice1.html
Super Spice Girls Page: www.jrfsm.demon.co.uk/spice_girls/index.html
Absolute Spice: www.abspice.home.ml.org
Say You'll Be There: www.geocities.com/SunsetStrip/Alley/7425
Spice Ring: www.kasst@iol.ie

There are thousands of great Spice Girls sites on the web. If these sites don't have what you want, just visit any search engine, type in Spice Girls and start surfing! You can join fan clubs, subscribe to newletters, see pictures, listen to audio clips, view video clips, and more....

BIBLIOGRAPHY

Cole, Annabel & Jackson, Ceri. "Revealed: How the Spice Girls Couldn't Sing a Note," *Daily Mail,* February 1997
Crowe, Jerry. "Spice and Everything Catchy," *The Los Angeles Times,* February 8, 1997
Flaherty, Mike. "Girls On Top," *Entertainment Weekly,* February 21-28, 1997
Golden, Anna Louise. *The Spice Girls: The Uncensored Story Behind Pop's Biggest Phenomenon*. NY: Ballantine Books, 1996
Gorman, Paul. "Taking on the British Pop Boys," *dotmusic,* April 1996
Pond, Steve. "Manufactured in Britain. Now Selling in America," *The New York Times,* February 16, 1997
Richardson, Julia. *All About the Spice Girls*. NY: Pocket Books, 1997
Spice Girls, Girl Power. Three Rivers Press, 1997
Spice Girls, Spice World: The Official Book of the Movie. Three Rivers Press, 1998
Baby Spice: In My Pocket. NY: Smithmark Books, 1997
Ginger Spice: In My Pocket. NY: Smithmark Books, 1997
Posh Spice: In My Pocket. NY: Smithmark Books, 1997
Sporty Spice: In My Pocket. NY: Smithmark Books, 1997
Scary Spice: In My Pocket. NY: Smithmark Books, 1997

PHOTO CREDITS

Alpha/Globe Photos, Inc.: ©Dave Benett: p. 68; ©Dave Parker: p. 74 bottom left

All Action/Retna Limited, U.S.A.: ©John Gladwin: p. 84; ©Dave Hogan: pp. 5 top, 5 bottom, 15; ©Doug Peters: pp. 58 bottom, 63, 79, 92; ©Nick Tansley: p. 2

Camerapress/Retna Limited, U.S.A.: ©David Dyson: pp. 7, 50 bottom, 53, 55, 78; ©Perou: pp. 52, 57, 72, 82; ©Mike Roberts: p. 88; ©Mark Stewart: p. 59

©Eric Catarina/Stills Press Agency/Retna Limited, U.S.A.: pp. 36-37

Globe Photos, Inc.: ©Steve Finn: p. 60

London Features International Limited: CAP: pp. 10-11, 44, 51, 76, 90; ©David Fisher: pp. 8-9, 14, 22-23, 32, 71, 80, 93;

©Gie Knaeps: p. 54; ©Colin Mason: pp. 34-35; ©Kevin Mazur: p. 83; ©Andy Phillips: p. 77 bottom right

Photofest: pp. 30-31, 33, 42-43, 85

Retna Limited, U.S.A.: ©Guy Aroch: p. 94; ©David Corio: pp. 16-17, 50 top, 58 top, 66 top; ©Steve Granitz: p. 13; ©Mick Hutson: pp. 24-25

Rex U.S.A. Limited: p. 95; ©David Abiaw: pp. 35 top right, 46 bottom left, 65; ©A.D. Crollalanza: p. 64; ©Dave Hogan: pp. 18-19, 20-21, 28-29, 45, 46-47, 67, 69, 74-75, 86, 89, 91 bottom left; ©Julian Makey: p. 48; ©Ken McKay: p. 70; ©Brian Rasic: pp. 38-39, 56, 66 bottom, 73; ©Tim Rooke: pp. 40, 61, 62; ©Dennis Stone: pp. 27 bottom left, 27 top right, 77 top left; ©Richard Young: pp. 6, 49, 81, 87, 91 top right